ALL GRANADA

Text, photographs, lay-out, design and printing by EDITORIAL ESCUDO DE ORO, S.A.
Rights of total or partial reproduction and translation reserved.
Copyright of this edition for photographs and text: © EDITORIAL ESCUDO DE ORO, S.A.
1st Edition, June 1993 - I.S.B.N. 84-378-1585-1 - Dep. Legal B. 16907-1993

Printed in EEC by FISA - Escudo de Oro, S.A.

Editorial Escudo de Oro, S.A.

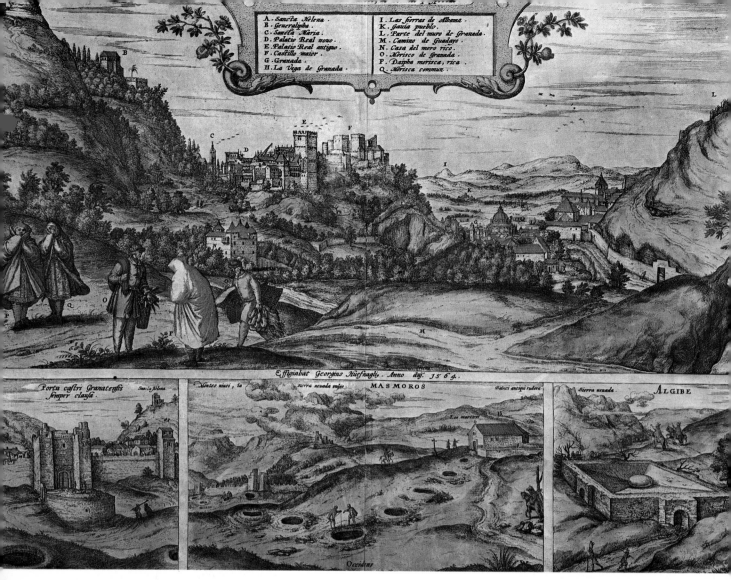

This 16th-century engraving, made not long after the end of the Moorish domination, shows the architectural elements which were, and still are for the most part, the most outstanding features of the city of Granada and its environs. Above and in the centre, the impressive outline of the Alhambra; on the right, the city, dominating the lovely fertile plain; and on the left, the splendid site of the Generalife. This delightful print, displayed in the Casa de los Tiros, is remarkable for the manner in which it illustrates the history of Granada.

FROM TURDULAN ILIVERIR TO MOSLEM GRANADA

It appears that the lands of Granda had contact with people from an advanced cilisation from prehistoric times.

The earliest historical records however relate to the Turdulos, one of the most civilised of the Iberian tribes and who produced coins on which Granada appears under the name *Iliverir*. Later came the Phoenicians, the Greeks and the Carthaginians. That the latter established themselves nearby in a large settlement has recently been confirmed by the discovery of an Iberian sculpture, the Dama de Baza, in the province of Granada.

The arrival of the Romans to the fertile plains around Granada marked the commencement of an important period in its history, and a Roman town, later the city of the Alhambra, was established. It was here that Saint Cecilio founded an Episcopal See in the year 62, and where, little more than two centuries later, the first Catholic Council in the entire Peninsula was constituted.

The Alhambra looks over the countryside with indolent Moorish majesty.

A fine night-time view of the Puerta del Vino and the towers of the Alcazaba.

Ancient *Ilíberis,* the Romanised version of Iberian *Iliverir,* grew in importance under the Visigoth monarchs, and reached the zenith of its splendour with the arrival of the Moors, whose entry into the City of the Darro was encouraged by the Jews established in the *Garnatha Alyehud* quarter.

THE ALHAMBRA

Around the middle of the 8th century, the Moors, already well established in the area, made the town of Castilia their capital and changed its name to Medina Elvira. It remained the capital of the province of Granada from the time of Omeya Abderramán to the reign of Zawí ben Zirí. But when the Caliphate of Cordova was in decline, corroded by internal struggles, Zawí ben Zirí, a valiant viceroy of the Omeyas, created a kingdom in the lands of Granada at the foot of the Sierra Nevada. Shortly afterwards, in the year 1013, the capital was moved to the site of the present city of Granada, and thus began a long period, containing moments of great splendour, which was ended by the Catholic Monarchs on 2 January 1492.

Granada grew and flourished under the rule of the Almorávides, who took over from the Ziris in the 11th century, and, later, under the Almohades. The result of these many years of Moorish rule was that the Moorish influence penetrated into every corner of the city.

The graceful contours of the Alhambra and the restrained architectual lines of the Palace of Carlos V stand amid the green countryside, forming part of the scene, and completing it.

The harmonious architecture of the horseshoe-shaped Moorish aXrch of the Puerta de la Justicia barely hints at the world of marvels which lies beyond.

The most glorious period of Mohammedan Granada began around the year 1236, when, on the fall of Cordova to the Christians, it became the capital of Moorish Spain. And it was precisely during this splendid chapter of the history of the city, marked by Moorish taste and refinement, that the architectural marvel that is the Alhambra was created.

The unmistakable outline of the Alhambra rises on a hill on the left bank of the River Darro. It stands opposite the site of ancient *Iliberia,* today occupied by the Albaicín and Alcazaba districts. This is a strategic point affording a wide view of the valleys of the Darro to the north and of the Assabica to the south, whilst to the east are the Cuesta del Rey Chico which, respectively, separate it from the Albaicín, Mount Mauror and the Cerro del Sol, crowned by the Generalife.

The Alhambra is surrounded by walls within which took place many of the bloody battles which form part of the history of the Kingdom of Granada. According to Arab chroniclers, the name «Alhambra» derives from the fact that the ancient fortress was rebuilt at night, by the reddish light of glowing torches. However, it appears more likely that the name comes from the colour the ferruginous soil on which the Alhambra is built gives to the walls, and that it is the combination of the Spanish version of two Arabic words, *calat alhamrá* - the red castle.

The *Alcazaba* was partially rebuilt by Savvar ben Hamdum in 889, and over the years it was repeatedly extended. By the 11th century, when the kings of the Zirí dynasty took up residence on the hill of the Albaicín, a wall had been buílt around the Alhambra Castle, which then became the most important fortress in the kingdom. Two centuries later, Mohammed ben Alahmar joined the palace with the fortress, marking the beginning of the most splendid period in the history of this site.

Climbing the hill up to the Alhambra by way of

The Puerta del Vino, leading to the Plaza de los Aljibes, retaining all its medieval elegance.

Cuesta de Gomérez, beginning at Plaza Nueva in the very centre of the city, the visitor is treated to magnificent views over the forest, which extends from the Puerta de las Granadas as far as the Palace of Carlos V, next to the Puerta de la Justicia, in Moorish times the main entrance to the fabulous city of the kings of Granada.

The Puerta de la Justicia has a huge Moorish arch, over whose keystone there is a carved hand. It is framed in bricks and has a voussoir lintel. This arch is the gateway into a defensive area, similar in function to machicolations in medieval times. Behind is the inner door, with another voussoir Moorish stone arch.in the abacuses bear the inscription «Praise to God. There is no God but Allah and Mohommad is His prophet. There is no strength but in God». In a recess in one of the walls is a statue of the Virgin with Child, and beyond the Puerta de la Justicia is a world which today exists only as a memory, but one which lives on in the beauty of this monument of exquisite art.

The Puerta de la Justicia also has a spacious hall, and the inner walls of the exit door are decorated with fine tiles.

Leaving behind the Puerta de la Justicia, one arrives at the Plaza de los Aljibes, with the Puerta del Vino, at which point the enchantment of the Alhambra begins to truly take hold of the visitor.

From the Plaza de los Aljibes, leaving to one side the Alcazaba and immediately opposite the Palace of Carlos V, one enters the Moorish palace, beginning what is certain to be a memorable visit to the Alhambra. In the Plaza de los Aljibes, we have already seen, from a magnificent belvedere over the city, a drama-tic panorama which will forever remain engraved on our memory: the Darro Valley, the Albaicín, the Sacromonte and the plains with, in the background, the slopes of the Sierra Nevada and Sierra Elvira, flanked by adjoining ranges of ragged

The cool elegance of the
Sala del Mexuar evokes
the feeling of the past
coming gracefully alive
once more.

An original view of the
Albaicín from one of the
magnificent belvederes
of the Alhambra.

Fragment of the mosaic in the Sala del Mexuar.

hills. In the words of the eminent Arabist García Gómez, «The Alhambra is not only the most beautiful but is also the most ancient of all the old Moorish palaces remaining in the world».

Once inside the Royal Alcázar, one feels that this would make the ideal setting for the «Thousand and One Nights». Whether the Mexuar (the Cuarto Dorado), the Serrallo (the Cuarto de Comares), or the Harem (the Cuarto de los Leones), there is always that same exquisite, perfumed atmosphere. Something intangible and ethereal emanates evocatively from these sumptuous halls consecrated by the grace of Moorish art.

The Mexuar

The Mexuar was the place where the kings of Granada granted audience to their citizens, and where burocracy was complied with and justice administered. Now partially demolished, it is impossible to form an idea of how it was originally as, apart from the restoration carried out under Yussuf I, a number of Christian elements were added here after the conquest of Granada by the Catholic Monarchs.

Palacio de Comares

Deeper into the interior of the Alhambra, we cross the Patio del Mexuar to arrive at the ancient residence of the Moorish kings, the *Serrallo* or the Cuarto de Comares. This is a palace of incomparable beauty and one of the most interesting and luxurious sites in the entire Alhambra. The delicate complexity of its decoration and ornamental richness is overwhelming, and the visitor becomes intoxicated by the rapture of such splendour. The polychromed tiles and filigreed plasterwork create a world of pure fantasy.

Through the door to the left, we come to the Patio de

The decoration of the Patio del Mexuar is like something out of the «Thousand and One Nights».

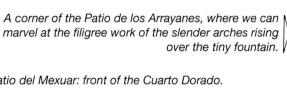

A corner of the Patio de los Arrayanes, where we can marvel at the filigree work of the slender arches rising over the tiny fountain.

Patio del Mexuar: front of the Cuarto Dorado.

los Arrayanes. Here air, light, water and foliage combine in joyful harmony with the architectural design to make this courtyard typical of the Alhambra in that all is subjugated to the pleasure of living, and each section is designed to give maximum delight to the senses. The Alhambra contains sections of particular loveliness, satisfying in every way with their grace and artistic harmony, and the Patio de los Arrayanes is certainly one of these privileged places.

The patio is a model of the typical courtyards to be found in Granada. Its grace, architectural balance and the intelligent use of natural elements combine to make a memorable picture of harmonious beauty. The distribution of the arches, if not decorated with such filigree, would remind one strongly of Greek architecture. The decoration of the roof of the north gallery, made of wood and partially destroyed by fire in 1890 is most impressive.

Leaving the Patio de los Arrayanes by the north side, we come to the Sala de la Barca, which was, it seems, originally decorated, though, unfortunately, little of this now remains. Lastly, the most monumental of the chambers in the royal palace: the Salón de Embajadores, in the Torre de Comares.

Torre de Comares and Salón de Embajadores

The Torre de Comares is the most impressive of the towers in the Alhambra, with a height of 45 metres and thick walls (2.5 metres) making clear its military function.

Inside is the Salón de Comares, or Salón de Embajadores, built by Yussuf I as his throne room, and hence the centre of political life and scene of all diplomatic negotiations.

Capital of one of the columns.

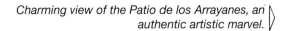

Another awe-inspiring view of the Patio de los Arrayanes, seen from the upper gallery.

The name «Comares» derives from the coloured glass windwos adorning the room, known as «qamariyyas» or «comarías».

The room is square, measuring 11.3 metres on each side, and is 18.2 metres high. The original floor was marble and it is certain to have had a fountain, like all the other rooms. At present, earthernware tiles alternate with 16th-century paving stones, culminating in a centre of glazed tiles from the same period, and bearing the coat of arms of the Alahmares. The huge number of openings, doors, windows, and nine balconies, determines the structure of the profuse decoration of the walls. The tiled socles, the complexity of the stuccos and the fine interlacing arches of the cedarwood ceiling, which still conserves hints of its former polychrome decoration, are evidence of the splendid past of the sumptuous Moorish court. The ornamental motifs are formed by the characteristic epigraphs, inlaid work and geometric figures of Moorish art, for this is an authentic jewel, a splendid, precise work of art. Formerly, the lighting was atenuated by thick curtains, beautiful plaster lattices and elegant *ajimeces* (projecting belvederes of wood and coloured glass) giving the room a mysterious, strongly Oriental air.

Palacio de los Leones

The Patio de los Leones was constructed by Mohammed V as private royal apartments, and is situated in the angle formed by the baths and the Patio de Comares, to which it runs perpendicular. It is a splendid example of Granadan Moorish art, reached by a narrow corridor connecting it with the Patio de los Arrayanes. The Patio de los Leones is formed by a huge central courtyard surrounded by galleries, with spacious rooms at one end. To the

Magnificent carving on the entrance door to the Sala de la Barca.

Salón de Embajadores.

The Albaicín and the Keep, seen from the Sala de Embajadores in the Torre de Comares.

north is the Sala de las Dos Hermanas, and behind it, the Sala de los Ajimeces and the Mirador de Daraxa. To the south is the Sala de los Abencerrajes, with the apartments forming the Harem. To the east is the Sala de los Reyes and to the west, the Sala de los Mocárabes.

The Patio de los Arrayanes communicates with the Cuarto de los Leones or Palacio del Harem through the Sala de los Mocárabes.

Sala de los Mocárabes.

This room is rectangular in shape, decorated with artistically adorned plasterwork, with religious inscriptions and the Nazari coat of arms and motto. Its original vault, discovered in the 19th century, adjoins that dating back to the 17th century. Crossing under three Mocarab arches, sustained by half-columns and capitals bearing inscriptions in praise of Mohammed V, we reach the Patio de los Leones.

The Patio de los Leones, with the fountain in the centre.

The Patio de los Leones, seen through the slender columns surrounding it.

The Patio de los Leones

The Patio de los Leones is perhaps the most popular and widely-known of the features of the Alhambra. It is in the centre of the buildings forming the Palace of the Harem, the private residence of the Nazarite kings and their retinues of wives, concubines and children.

The solid appearance of the twelve lions grouped round the stylised fountain in the centre contrasts strongly with the apparent fragility of the rest of the Alhambra. The architectural design of this courtyard is, simply, the work of genius. It is splendidly adorned with 124 slender columns around the edges, worthy of admiration, as is everything in this unique, incomparable marvel.

The ancient basin of the fountain is made of white marble and around it are carved a lovely dedication by the poet Aben Zemrec for Mohammed V, during whose reign the Palace of the Harem was built: «By good fortune, in this garden have we not got something which God himself could not have wished more beautiful? It is decorated with splendid pearls, with more around the base as if they had overflowed from the fountain. The silver water gushes among these jewels, contrasting with the beauty of the gleaming white marble». Among the buildings forming the Harem, grouped around this marvellous courtyard are the Sala de los Mocárabes, the Sala de los Abencerrajes, the Salón de los Reyes and the Sala de las Dos Hermanas (with the Sala de los Ajimeces and the Mirador de Daraxa). From the Patio de los Leones we can also visit the royal cemetery, from where Boabdil, last king of Granada,

A view
through the
filigreed
arches
showing the
fountain,
guarded by
lions.

The Sala de
los
Abencerrajes,
scene of
tragic events
in the
Alhambra
during
Moorish
times.

A delightful painting decorating the ceiling in the Sala de los Reyes.

disenterred the remains of his forefathers, transferring them to Mondújar.

Sala de los Abencerrajes

This is situated opposite the Sala de las Dos Hermanas, and takes its name from the legend that it was here that the noble Abencerrajes were put to the sword. There is a double entrance arch, with three double arches finely decorated, supported by columns with blue capitals. The walls are also richly adorned, restored in the 16th century. The Mocarab dome is a work of admirable beauty.

Decoration on the ceiling of the Sala de los Abencerrajes.

Majestic view of the Sala de los Reyes.

cent paintings decorating the ceiling, depicting ten Moors, seated in conversation on a gilded background with decorative elements in relief, and coats of arms sustained by lions. The paintings would appear to represent the ten first sultans of the Nazari dynasty, and are thought to date back to the late-14th or early-15th centuries.

These lively-coloured but simply-drawn figures are reminiscent of Chinese painting, or of the illustrations on Persian manuscripts. What would appear to comprise further evidence to their Moorish origin is their similarity as regards preparation and execution to those found in Berber countries, particulary Morocco. A notable feature is that they were painted on animal hides sewn together and then stuck to the wood of the vault.

Sala de las Dos Hermanas

This room was constructed at the end of the reign of Mohammed V and is a square measuring eight metres along each side. Its name comes from the large twin tiles on the marble floor, flanking the central fountain.

The room is adorned with semicircular arches at each end. The side arches provide access to small rooms with ornate ceilings.

The walls of the Sala de las Dos Hermanas are covered by fine plasterwork on different themes, resembling filigree. Most appear characteristic of 14th-century Moorish art. The tiles of the socle, of metallic hues, are interesting, as some of the enamel has such unusual colours in such work as violet. However, the most impressive element is the hon-

Sala de los Reyes

Also known as the Sala de la Justicia, this forms the eastern end of the Patio de los Leones and is a rectangle measuring 31 metres by 7 metres. The room is entered by three porches with triple arches supported by fine columns decorated with entertwined geometric shapes. The Sala de la Justicia is divided into three sections, separated by robust double arches. The rectangular compartments formed by these arches are covered by ornate vaults. Various alcoves open at the end of the room, decorated with inscriptions in praise of God and Mohammed V. This is one of the most interesting interior in the entire Alhambra, containing magnifi-

The splendid filigree wook in the Mirador de Lindaraja gives it the appearance of a rich jewel box.

eycomb dome, which appears to the visitor as if it were a vault defying gravity, sustained in space by magic. It is supported by the octagonal form of its base, on similarly honeycombed squinches.

The apartments above were probably used by the women who, behind wooden lattices, could thus witness festivities and entertainments.

Sala de los Ajimeces

Its name derives from the *ajimeces*, or small balconies, in its north side, overlooking the gardens. The honecomb vault was restored between 1537 and 1541 by the Morisco Francisco de las Maderas. Half

the walls are covered by plasterwork with religious inscriptions, and a coat of arms with Nazari motto. A large honeycombed pointed arch in the middle of the back wall gives access to the Mirador de Daraxa, a delightful work of Moorish art.

Mirador de Daraxa

This is, without doubt, one of the masterpieces of the Alhambra. The room is, in fact, the first of the Harem apartments, and is decorated with exquisite delicacy, as are all the adjoining rooms, destined for use by the sultana.

The Sala de los Baños, also known as the Sala del Reposo.

Its Moorish name, «l-ain-dar-aixa» («eyes of the sultana») makes completely clear that it was used by the sultana to contemplate the beautiful views which stretched out before her as far as the Darro Valley, before the construction of the Charles V rooms. The windows are very low, as the Moors generally sat on cushions placed on the floor.

The walls are decorated delicately and with unsurpassed beauty, so richly as to resemble the finest ivory work. The inscriptions for the most part reproduce verses by Aben Zemrec. The interior of the belvedere is formed by a tiny rectangular room with a pair of side arches and one double arch in the centre. The windows are adorned by pointed honeycomb arches.

The tiled socle, of great beauty and complexity, combines black, white and yellow, ending with a tiny inscription.

The coffered ceiling is made of wood and formerly contained coloured glass.

Royal Baths

These are found to the east of the Palacio de Comares, its structure resembling that of Roman baths. The Sala de las Camas contains four columns supporting brackets and lintels, forming a square area in the centre, with a fountain surrounded by galleries. The walls are richly decorated in a variety of colours, most of this work dating back to Christian times. The floor is by Francisco de las Maderas, made in the workshop of Isabel de Robles between 1541 and 1542.

From here, we enter the baths, contemplating the fine architectural forms, and the plain walls. The baths have white marble floors, tiled socles, smooth Moorish arches and magnificent vaults from which chandaliers hang. A segmental arch permits entry to the central room.

The Partal Gardens, restored with absolute respect for the design of the original, are surrounded by interesting monuments with outlines of purely Moorish origin, reflected in the waters of the central pool.

The most important part of the buildings in this section of the Alhambra is, without doubt, El Partal or, as it is more usually known, the Torre de las

Detail of the Sala del Reposo, showing the fine plasterwork

El Partal.

Damas. This tower rises over the gardens, proudly surveying the surrounding countryside. It is said that it was from this tower that Boabdil escaped after confronting his father, Muley Abul Hasán, who was bewitched by the beauty of Zoraya. Its original name -it has also been known as *Torre del Príncipe,* or *Baño de las Odaliscas-* comes from the porch -partal- formed by the five access arches.

The gallery of the Torre de las Damas has an ornamental wood ceiling with original decoration. In the centre is a cupola adorned with stars, small domes and curved shells. Six small balconies open out at one end of the gallery, which has triple arches on each side. A large arch, richly decorated, pro-vides access to the room, which has three windows on each side. From this belvedere, the highest part of the tower, is a delightful view of the Darro Valley. Two large stone lions stand guard beside the pool. The visitor leaves the Torre de las Damas, whose construction is believed to date from the early-14th century, filled with melancholy.

To the right of the Torre de las Damas is that of El Mihrab, the parapet of the wall serving as its base. The façade is in the form of a horseshoe arch, and the tower contains an unusual Moorish oratory.

After inspecting the Torre de los Picos, built to defend one of the entrances to the Generalife, the Torre del Cadí, and that of Las Infantas, one may

The silhouettes of the cypress trees lend a melancholy air to this view of El Partal.

stop to admire the Torre de la Cautiva (of the Captive) built by Yusuf I. It has delicate plasterwork, and evokes the romantic figure of Isabel de Solís, no other than the lovely Zoraya, whose poetic legend lingers on throughout the Alhambra. After contemplating this marvel of Moorish art, committing its form to memory, it may help to dispel our confused feelings by inspecting the front of the former Monastery of San Francisco, a Moorish palace dating back to the late-14th century and now a Parador (national hotel). In the high chapel were once buried the Catholic Monarchs.

Morisca houses in El Partal.

The Renaissance front of the Palace of Carlos V impresses due to the strength of its architectural design.

THE PALACE OF CARLOS V

Among the many fine buildings over which the Alhambra presides is the Renaissance Palace of Carlos V, one of the most remarkable. Building commenced in 1527 under Pedro Machuca, and the palace was destined to be the residence of the emperor, who had a special fondness for Granada. The work, however, had to be suspended in 1568, due to the Moorish rebellion, and was not resumed until 1579. The palace is in the form of a quadrangle and has an air of serene majesty. It is considered the most beautiful Renaissance palace outside Italy.

The south front boasts a magnificent porch, decorated by the sculptor Nicolao da Corte, and the west front featueres some equally fine carvings by Juan de Orea.

The central courtyard is circular and impressively large, surrounded by a spacious portico of 32 Doric columns contrasting with the Ionic columns of the upper gallery.

To go from the ethereal and romantic atmosphere of the Alhambra to the classical restraint of the Palace of Carlos V is a rich, rewarding experience.

*The orginal
circular
courtyard in
the Palace
of Carlos V.*

A finely-carved stone water trough, one of the most valuable treasures in the collections of the National Museum of Spanish-Moorish Art, housed in the Palace of Carlos V.

THE NATIONAL MUSEUM OF SPANISH-MOSLEM ART

This museum is housed on the ground floor of the Palace of Carlos V and contains a rich collection of Moorish and Mudéjar art. Perhaps the most important exhibit is the famous Alhambra Pitcher, which was for many years displayed in the Sala de las dos Hermanas. The Moorish grace of its form is equalled only by the delicacy of its decoration.

The 11th-century stone trough is another valuable piece, with magnificent reliefs depicting lions and antelopes fighting at the foot of a tree. The tombs, capitals, arches and ceramic work contained in this museum are also of great interest.

Other outstanding Moorish works include a fine dish illustrated with a bird mounted on a horse, from Medina Elvira, and a pair of engraved, embossed gold bracelets.

The museum also contains an interesting collection of Visigoth art, such as bronze and silver bracelets and earrings, delicate glass and amber necklaces, rings, 4th- and 5th-century bronze clasps, and a number of Corinthian capitals.

THE PROVINCIAL FINE ARTS MUSEUM

This museum is on the first floor of the Palace of Carlos V, where it was transferred from the Casa de Castril, which belonged to Hernando de Zafra, secretary to the Catholic Monarchs.

The present site of the museum is fitted to its function, and very spacious. It was opened in 1958 and consists of eleven rooms and entrance and exit halls, together housing a rich and varied picture gallery and a valuable collection of sculptures.

One of the most important works contained here is the central panel of the Triptych of the Gran Capitán, a fine 15th-century enamel from Limoges attributed to Nardon Penicaud.

The paintings include a number of larger canvasses dealing with religious subjects, by Juan de Sevilla, some fine works by Pedro Antonio Bocanegra, a

The Toledan Swordsmith, a work of vigorous naturalism by Mariano Fortuny.

After work, an expressive painting by Martínez Cubells.

Triptych of the Gran Capitán, a magnificent work in raised enamel.

The magnificent Jarrón de la Alhambra, *in the Granadan Museum of Spanish and Moorish Art.*

Virgen con el Niño en brazos, a fine carving by Diego de Siloé.

panel of the Virgin and Child (15th-century Spanish-Flemish art), a notable collection of works by Sánchez Cotán and an interesting variety of works by unknown painters.

19th-century art is represented by works by Madrazo, Muñoz Degrain, Gómez Moreno, Pérez Villamil, Vicente López, Carlos Haes, Moreno Carbonero,

A splendid Flemish tapestry, hanging in one of the halls of the Museum of Granada.

The fine jets of water from the fountains, the flowers, the myrtle trees and the cypresses all blend to give the gardens of the Generalife their melancholy air.

José Larrocha, Emilio Sala, Fortuny and Martínez Cubells.

Among 20th-century artists, the best represented are Rodríguez Acosta, Luis Mosquera, Roberto Domingo, Gómez Mir, Soria Aedo and Vázquez Díaz.

Of particular interest is the Salon of the Italian Chimney-piece. This is a spacious room in which restraint and good taste over decoration result in perfect harmony. The room takes its name from the fine marble chimney-piece, a 16th-century Italian work originally made for the Palace of Carlos V.

There are many fine sculptural exhibits in this museum, such as the large decorated carving on wood, the «Burial of Christ», by Jacobo Florentino. Other important pieces include: «Virgin and Child», a polychrome carving attributed to Roberto Alemán, the «Virgin with Child» by Diego Siloé, the splendid «Head of Saint John of God», by Alonso Cano, the moving «Ecce Homo», by Pedro de Mena, the four large sculptures carved by Alonso Cano and Pedro de Mena, «Saint Matthew», by Juan de Orea and «The Child Christ at Prayer», by Risueño.

Entrance to the Patio de la Acequía, in the Generalife.

The poetically-beautiful gardens of the Generalife.

Overall view of the Patio de la Acequia.

THE GENERALIFE

The palace and gardens of the Generalife are emplaced on the slopes of the Cerro del Sol, commanding a fine view, dominated by the city itself, of the Darro and Genil valleys.

The Generalife was formerly the pleasure palace of the monarchs of Granada, its name deriving, it appears, from *Gennat-Alarif,* meaning «garden of the architect». It was probably built in the mid-13th century, but has since then been altered several times.

The beauty and enchantment of these gardens are unrivalled, the winding paths evocative and poetic. The Paseo de los Cipreses and the Paseo de las

The southern section of the Patio de los Surtidores.

Adelfas are two such which seem to lead to some romantic haven.

Here in the Patio de la Acequia, the scent of flowers and the soft murmuring of the water bubbling from the fountains produce the illusion of being in a fairy-tale land.

The ethereal outline of the little palace is reflected in the waters of the pools, and a dusky grace flitters among the arches, rooms, galleries and plaster latticework. The decoration is rich and elegant, the surrounding landscape making its presence felt through the numerous belvederes.

The design of the Generalife gardens is highly individual, with an unusual layout delineated by an enchanting labyrintyh of bowers, fountains, flower beds, a veritable paradise of geraniums, carnations and green hedges of box and cypress.

The Alhambra, seen from the Generalife.

«The Surrender of Granada», a famous work by Pradilla.

THE CHAPEL ROYAL

Following the entrance of the Catholic Monarchs into Granada on 2 January 1492, an artistic and cultural movement of the first order began in the city. This was the Renaissance whose ideas were splendidly transferred to the Kingdom of Granada. The special warmth which Isabel always felt towards this city made her decide, according to the royal decree she signed in Medina del Campo on 13 September 1504, to build the famous Chapel Royal as a sepuchre for herself and her husband. Work began in 1506 under the direction of Enrique Egas, by which time the Queen had already died and her remains been laid to rest in the Monastery of San Fernando. King Ferdinand took special interest in complying with his deceased wife's wishes, and on his death on 23 January 1516 his body was taken to lie beside that of his queen in the same monastery. On 10 November 1521, the remains of both were taken to the Chapel Royal, where their tombs can be seen to this day.

The chapel is built in Toledan style, with a pronounced Gothic influence, and is a typical example of architecture during the reign of the Catholic Monarchs.

Outside, the chapel has just one façade, due to the fact that on the other three sides the building adjoins the walls of the cathedral, the Church of the Sagrario and the Lonja (Exchange).

The original entrance to the Chapel Royal, now in Granada Cathedral.

The front is restrained in style, with a Plateresque portico. The walls, flanked by buttresses ending in decorative pinnacles, support pierced balustrades with fine crests. The poised elegance of the great windows and the gargoyles combines harmoniously with the shields and emblems of the Catholic Monarchs, which embellish the front.
The transept is enclosed by an artistic Plateresque gilded wrought-iron grille, a fine example of the work of Bartolomé de Jaén. Behind this grille are the royal

A view of the exterior and main entrance to the Chapel Royal.

Statues of the Catholic Monarchs at prayer, in the sacristy of the Chapel Royal. Coffins of the Catholic Monarchs.

The crown, sceptre and coffer of Isabel the Catholic, and the sword of Ferdinand.

The Lonja, or Exchange.

The Triptych of the Passion, by Dierick Bouts.

Tombs of the Catholic Monarchs and Juana the Mad and Philip the Handsome, carved in fine marble from Carrara.

The Plateresque reredos over the high altar, one of the first in this style, by Felipe de Vigarny.

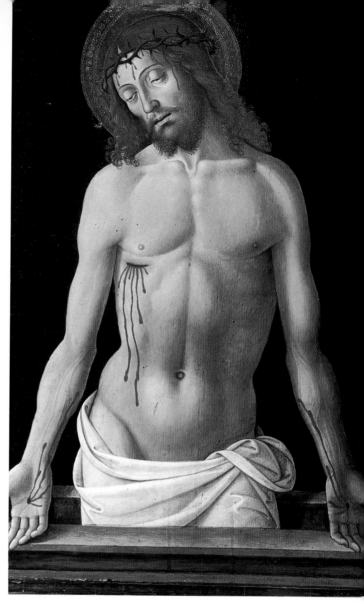

Oracion del Huerto, a delicate painting by Botticelli handing in the picture gallery of the Chapel Royal in Granada.

Cristo, a fine work by Perugino.

tombs, sculpted in Carrara marble. Beside them are the tombs of Philip the Handsome and Juana the Mad, daughter of the Catholic Monarchs.

The four bodies, with that of Michael, the child prince, lie below in the crypt, enclosed in impressively austere metal coffins.

The magnificent reredos behind the High Altar is by Vigarny, and was one of the first Plateresque altar screens to be made in Spain. Various additions have been made to it in Gothic style.

The other two altars are also interesting, and have altarpieces in the form of cubboards, which contain the relics donated by several popes to the Catholic Monarchs, since then kept here.

Since 1945, the chapel treasure has been housed in the sacristy, presided over by a 16th-century figure of Christ, at whose feet are statues of the kneeling Catholic Monarchs. The treasure includes jewels of immense value, the crown and sceptre of Isabel and the sword of Ferdinand.

Other outstanding pieces are the Queen's Coffer, which according to tradition once held the jewellery

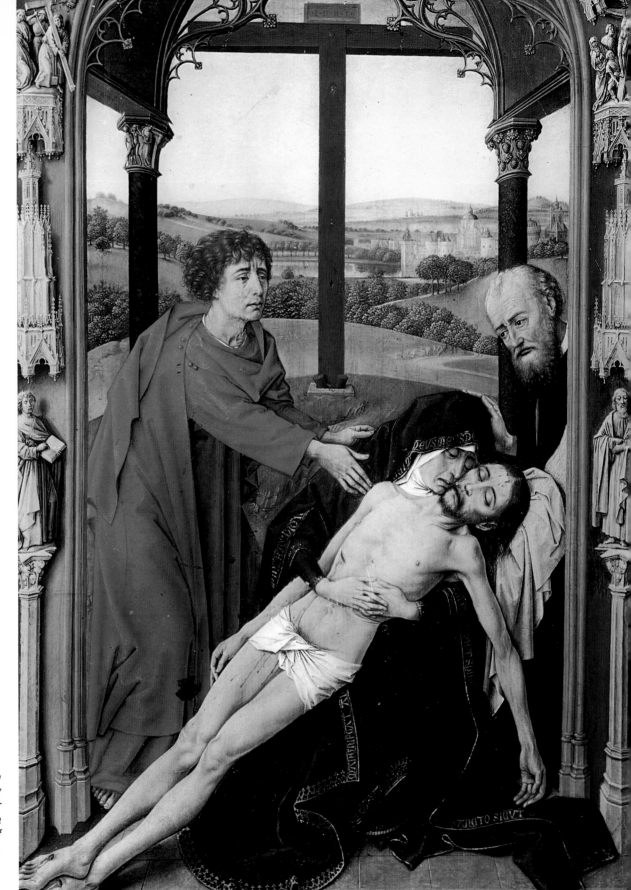

Cristo muerto, by Van der Weyden, a painting of deep pathos.

sold to help finance the voyage of Columbus, her gilded silver mirror, now converted into a monstrance, an altar cross, a chalice with engraved decoration and a splendid pyx with relief work in marble.
There is also a fine collection of paintings by Botticelli, Perugino, Van de Weyden, Memling, Bouts, Berruguete and Bosch.

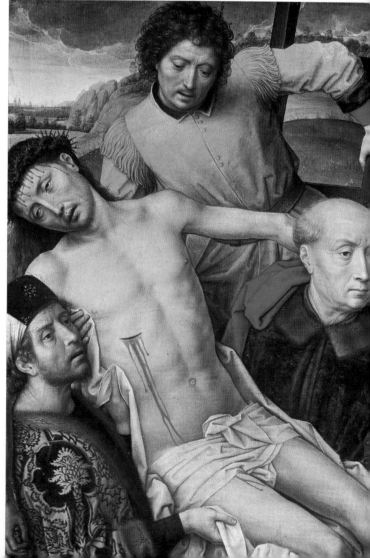

Saint John, an original vision by Berruguete.

Descent from the Cross, by Memling

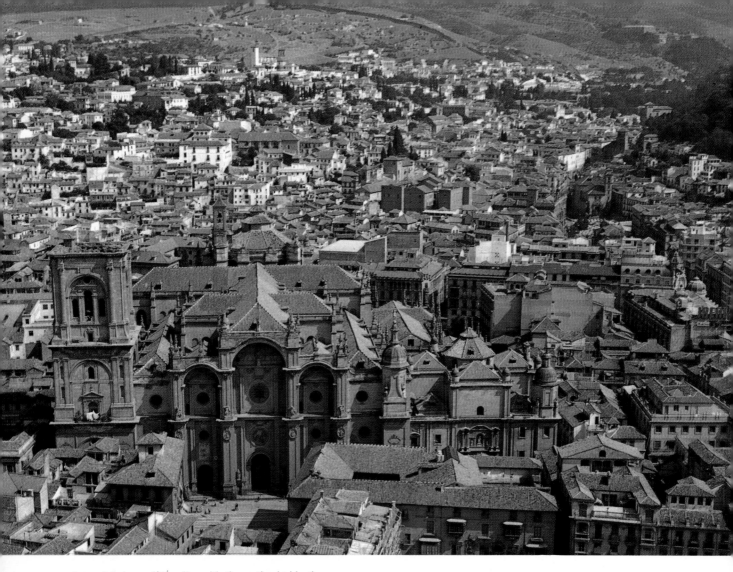

An aerial view of the city, with the cathedral in the foreground.

THE CATHEDRAL

Around four months after the conquest of Granada by the Christian armies, the first cathedral in the city was established in the Mosque of the Alhambra. Later, this was transferred to the Monastery of San Francisco, and later still it was decided to construct a cathedral beside the Great Mosque, by then converted into the Church of Santa María de la O. Work began in 1518. At first, it was to be in Gothic style, similar to Toledo Cathedral, but this project was finally abandoned, and in 1528 Diego Siloé took charge, directing work until his death in 1563.

The main front is by Alonso Cano, who modified and simplified the original plans drawn up by Siloé.

The cathedral impresses by the grandeur of its architecture. A surprising feature of its design is that over a Gothic groundplan has been constructed a Renaissance building, without affecting the overall harmony of the site.

The main chapel of the cathedral, one of Siloé's major works.

The Virgen de Belén, a delicious sculpture by Alonso Cano.

Head of Saint John the Baptist, by Ruiz del Peral.

The interior is magnficent, consisting of a nave and four aisles, all huge, whilst the sides of the building are lined with chapels containing fine altarpieces and works by Alonso Cano, Torrigiano, Bocanegra and Ribera.

The entire interior is filled with light from the many windows. The stained glass is of great beauty, particularly the seven Flemish windows by Teodoro of Holland, depicting scenes from the life of the Virgin, and the three featuring the Holy Parents, by Jan Campen.

The white walls of the cathedral contrast sharply with the shining gold of the high chapel, the masterly work of Diego de Siloé. On the Plateresque columns of the main arch are the statues of the Catholic Monarchs at prayer, carved by Pedro de Mena and Medrano. A little higher up are two busts of Adam and Eve, sculpted by Alonso Cano and polychromed by Vélez de Ulloa.

Inmaculada, by Alonso Cano.

The Puerta del Perdón, the finest of the cathedral entrances.

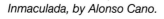

*The dazzling
Gilded
Chapel in the
cathedral.*

The interior of the cathedral is filled with majestic light.

A study of the magnificent reredos in the Church of San Jerónimo.

Statues of the Gran Capitán and his wife, María Manrique, at prayer, in the Monastery of San Jerónimo.

The beautiful Plateresque entrance to the Carthusian Monastery.

THE MONASTERY OF SAN JERONIMO

Founded by the Catholic Monarchs in Santa Fe in 1492, the Monastery of San Jerónimo was dedicated to Saint Catherine and transferred to Granada. Work on the building began in 1496 and was completed under the direction of Siloé in 1547. The Catholic Monarchs donated all the Arab stone from Elvira used in the construction.

The monastery, which formerly contained many valuable ornaments, was sacked by the French and later converted into barracks, but some years ago was restored, with the co-operation of the University of Granada and the Order of Saint Jerome. The courtyards and gardens of the site are exceptionally beautiful, as are the cloisters. The front of the church features unusual decoration by Siloé. It consists of the coat of arms of the Catholic Monarchs beneath a window encased in an arch with carvings of fantastic animals. Over the four Doric columns of the porch is a small shrine with a statue of Saint Francis.

The reredos in the main chapel is excellent, extending from the front of the apse to the vault and consisting of four sections supported by a *sotobanco* with a number of fine carvings.

View of the cloisters.

The refectory, built in the mid-16th century.

The lay choirstalls, with two splendid paintings by Sánchez Cotán.

A partial view of the sacristy, showing its rich decoration.

THE CARTHUSIAN MONASTERY

Situated on the outskirts of the city, the Carthusian Monastery (La Cartuja) is a harmonious construction with an attractive Plateresque porch predating both the Chapel Royal and the Lonja. It has a semicircular arch bearing the coats of arms of Spain. Pillars on either side support a simply-decorated cornice, over which, in an embellished vaulted niche is a 16th-century wood carving of the Virgen.

Behind this is the church and a large courtyard, whilst at one side is the Monastery entrance, reached by stairs carved in Elvira stone.

The walls of the Claustrillo, a delightful courtyard with Doric arches, were originally decorated with paintings by Vicente Carducho and Sánchez Cotán, but these have now been placed in the refectory.

Between the two altars is an unusual door inlaid with ivory, shells and rare woods.

The two choirs, the monks' and lay choirs, are communicated by a fine door, and exhibit paintings by Bocanegra and Sánchez Cotán, featuring religious themes.

In the refectory, one's attention is ceased by the Gothic vaults and by a cross painted on a rock by Sánchez Cotán, who also painted the altarpiece in the *Sala de Profundis*.

The church is built entirely of stone. Behind the altar and the chancel, which acts as the sanctuary, is the outstanding Sancta Sanctorum, with a vividly-decorated Baroque shrine. A door on the left leads to the sacristy, completed in 1764. This is a room of subtle lines, a maximum exponent of the Baroque style, with an audacious combination of decorative elements.

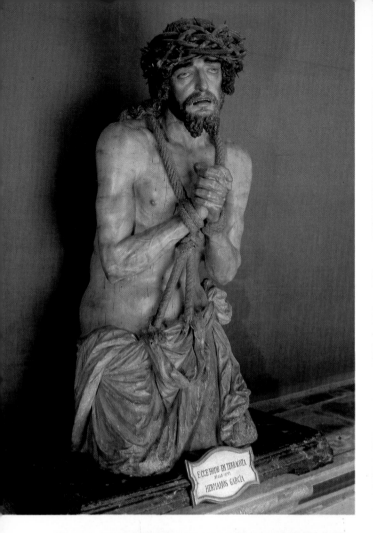

Terracotta Ecce Homo, attributed to the García brothers, in the Carthusian Monastery.

The Virgin of the Rosary, by Bocanegra, also in the Carthusian Monastery.

St Bruno, a magnificent figurine by José de Mora (Carthusian Monastery).

THE HOSPITAL OF SAN JUAN DE DIOS

The hospital stands beside the Church of San Juan de Dios and occupies the former Monastery of San Jerónimo, a fine example of Spanish Renaissance architecture, founded by the Catholic Monarchs in 1492. It was transferred to its present site in 1504.

The Nursing Order of Saint John founded the hospital, which features a fine portico with Doric columns and a magnificent ceiling over the staircase. Standing in the Calle de San Juan de Dios, its life and work are closely linked with that of the city of Granada.

The magnificent courtyard of the Hospital of San Juan de Dios, with the beautiful arches on the sides.

This painting by Gómez-Moreno symbolises the spirit which illuminated the life and work of Saint John of God.

This view of the dazzling beauty of the High Chapel of the Church of San Juan de Dios shows all the richness of its ornamentation.

THE CHURCH OF SAN JUAN DE DIOS

Building began in 1737 and the church was consecrated in 1759. It is one of the most beautiful places of worship in Granada. The façade is surmounted by two high towers topped by spires, and has an entrance made of marble from the Sierra Elvira, with mahogany doors designed by José Bada, and two series of columns supported by pedestals. One section of these is composed of Corinthian columns, whilst the other features Composite columns. In the centre of the upper section is a statue of Saint John of God by Ramiro Ponce de León. The church has a Latin cross groundplan. Inside are four chapels, a choir and a high dome over the transept.

The high chapel features an impressive gilded reredos by J.F. Guerrero. Its splendid decoration includes a shrine in the centre, combined with a profusion of reliefs, paintings, marble ornamentation and mirrors.

The façade of the Church of San Juan de Dios, with its Baroque entrance and its spired towers.

An overall view of Granada, with the cathedral in the centre.

THE CITY

The passing of time has had a profound effect on the city of Granada. It has been the meeting-place of different cultures and a melting-pot of races and religions, whilst economic and social changes have also left their mark. The great events of history it has witnessed, and the city's geographic position, have conditioned and helped to mould the character of the people of Granada. They are more reserved and quiet than Andalusians generally, but their charac-

ter is also enriched by a certain courtesy. Théofile Gautier, the French writer enamoured of the glow and fire of the people of Andalusia, lived in Granada for some years, in Calle Párraga, where he forged his artistic talent.

Granada is one of the loveliest cities in Spain, and enjoys a pleasant climate, the logical consequence of its ideal position overlooking a fertile plain, almost at the very foot of the Sierra Nevada. As García Lorca said, *«The two rivers of Granada flow down from the snow to the grain».*

*A view of a
peaceful
street
leading to
the
cathedral
and the
Chapel
Royal.*

Façade of La Madraza.

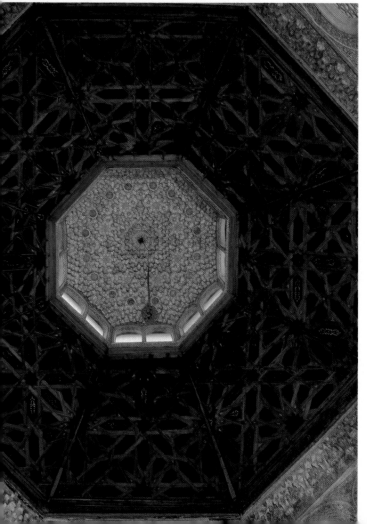

Coffered ceiling of the oratory in the Moorish Room in La Madraza.

Modern Granada extends over the plains, whereas the old town with its Jewish and Moorish roots formerly clung to the hills, dominated by the Alhambra.

The city centre is formed by the intersection of two main thoroughfares, the Gran Vía de Colón (which leads to the street containing the Chapel Royal and the cathedral) and the Avenida de los Reyes Católicos.

It is a real pleasure to lose onself in any of the delightful side streets of Granada, such as the purely Moorish Alcaicería -pure Moorish filigree- or the Zacatín, or to relax in the popular Plaza de Bibarrambla. Other pleasant spots are the Plaza de Isabel la Católica, at the junction of Calle de los Reyes Católicos and Gran Vía de Colón, with its fine fountain and statue of Isabel I and, further down, Calle Angel Ganviet, named after the ill-fated local born writer, author of the famous «Idearium Español».

Detail of the oratory in the
Moorish Room (La Madraza).

The oratory in the Moorish Room
(La Madraza).

The Knights' Room.

The Virgin of the Rose, by an
unknown artist.

Plaza Nueva.

The Fountain of Triumph at dusk.

Monument to Isabel the Catholic and Columbus.

Partial view of Plaza de Bibarrambla.

The beautiful courtyard at the Royal Hospital.

Two delightful nooks in the gardens of the Fundación Rodríguez Acosta, near the Palace of Carlos V.

The Casa de Castril. The doorway, though attributed to Siloé, is more likely to be the work of Sebastián de Alcántara.

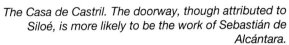

The banks of the River Darro, immortalised by Lorca.

The coat of arms of Granada, with its unique embroidery.

The aristocratic chimney-piece in the Sessions Chamber.

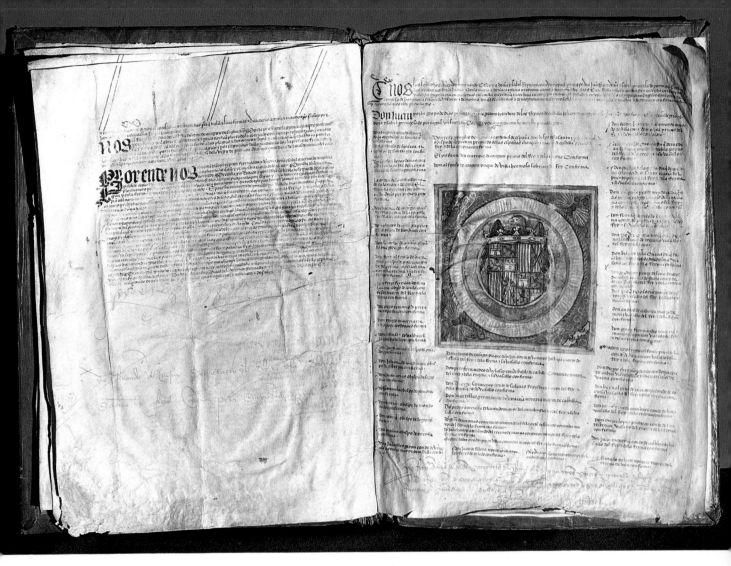

The Treaty of Surrender, signed by Boabdil.

THE CITY HALL (AYUNTAMIENTO)

Nowadays, Granada City Hall is housed in part of the Monastery of Carmelitas Calzadas which survived the dissolution. The building has been altered several times, and in 1910 was extended as fara as Calle de los Reyes Católicos.

Inside the building, whose centre is occupied by the original courtyard of the monastery, is an interesting Historical Museum, founded in 1939. It contains the treaty of the surrender of Granada by the Moors, signed by the Catholic Monarchs, as well as the coat of arms of the city, beautifully embroidered and donated by Isabel to the City Council in 1493. Other items include the Royal Standard of Granada, with the coat of arms of the House of Austria embroidered on carmine damask, a 16th-century tapestry depicting the Virgin Mary, a copy of the Gothic edition of the city ordenances, the patents by which Isabel II awarded the name «heroic» to the city, and a number of fine silver objects.

The museum also exhibits a small wooden chest, adorned with allegorical carvings, in which lie the mortal remains of Mariana Pineda, the Granadan

The fine craft work of Granada, going back to Moorish times and continuing until the present, has a worldwide reputation. Here are four examples: pottery, marquetry, rug-making and guitar manufacture.

The original front of the House of Los Tiros shows that it was formerly a fortress.

maid who inspired one of Lorca's first plays, as well as the manuscript of Zorrilla's poem, «The Gnomes of the Alhambra».

Among the paintings is one by Juan Leandro de la Puente, signed in 1639 and depicting the Feast of Pentecost, a crucifixion and a *Pietà* by Gómez-Moreno, a portrait of Isabel II by Soledad Enríquez, one of Mariana Pineda by J. Lozano, another of Alfonso XII by Madrazo, portraits of Castelar, Cánovas del Castillo and Sagasta by Gómez-Moreno, and other valuable works by Isidoro Marín, José María Mezquita and Gabriel Morcillo.

The Municipal Archives have a very interesting collection of historical documents which enable one to follow step by step the illustrious course of history in Christian Granada. There are the Minute Books, dating back to 1497 onwards, as well as thirteen books of Privileges and Royal Letters Patent from 1490 on, with the signatures of the Catholic Monarchs and successive kings and queens of great historic value. The wide Avenida de los Reyes Católicos nearby lends an additional air of importance to the City Hall.

CASA DE LOS TIROS

Standing in Plaza del Padre Suarez, the House of los Tiros, formerly the Palace of the Princes of Granada, contains the Museum of History and Handicrafts of Granada.

The building has the appearance of a fortress, and it is said that it originally formed part of the walls protecting the Alfareros district.

The present house was built in the first half of the 16th century. The entire front is of stone, and ends in a square fortified tower crowned by battlements, and a roof, added during the 19th century.

There is a simple doorway, with a lintel in the centre, balconies and five statues of Hercules, Theseus,

Jason, Hector and Mercury. The statue of the Mercury bears the coat of arms of the house.

The ground floor is occupied by a spacious, magnificent entrance hall, the huge beams of ceiling supported by Gothic lintels.

There is a small courtyard with a number of Moorish capitals and columns. The most interesting room is, without a doubt, the main chamber, which retains its original architectural purity, with finely carved beams and lintels with beautiful reliefs. Four stone medallions, with busts in high relief, decorate the upper section of the walls, and the doors contain Plateresque carvings.

The treasure in the House of Los Tiros is a varied collection accumulated by Antonio Gallego y Burín, an illustrious son of the city who was Director-General of Fine Arts, and whose portrait now hangs in one of the rooms of this building. Throughout the

Coffered ceiling of the Golden Hall in the House of Los Tiros.

The world of the Gypsies also has its special place in the House of Los Tiros where it seems that, in the words of Lorca, «Sobre el rostro del aljibe se mecía la gitana».

house, one can sense the subtle presence of the soul of Granada and the complex and unique personality of a city steeped in history. On the ground floor, beside the courtyard, is a kitchen in the Alpujarras style, with a typical hearth adorned with ceramics and other household utensils, forming an example of the interior of an inn during the times of the Duke of San Pedro de Galatino. Another room contains bull-fighting trophies connected with the city, and an interesting album of press cuttings dating back to 1764 onwards.

On the floor above, the museum offers a wide range of artistic and historical works of various kinds. Outstanding and contrasting personalities of Granada are represented, for example: the Empress Eugenia, who has a room dedicated to her memory; Mariana Pineda, of whom there is a portrait and a

Terracotta figures in the Gypsy Room

Façade of the City Hall.

Parador de San Francisco, Palacio de los Córdoba, royal chambers of Santo Domingo and the front of the Provincial Deputation.

series of three pictures illustrating her progress towards execution at the scaffold; and Chorroejumo, King of the Gypsies, the writers Martínez de la Rosa and Pedro Antonio Alarcón, and General Alvarez de Castro, who defended Gerona against Napoleon, of whom there are portraits.

There is also a room dedicated to Washington Irving, the American writer who lived in Granada. This room contains many editions of his work, «Tales of the Alhambra», as well as a library of books about the Alhambra by Spanish and foreign authors. Another room, a dining-room in Spanish style, contains a magnificent colection of Granadan ceramic.

These pieces are hung on the walls, and the entire room is arranged with excellent good taste, giving a balanced view of the decorative arts of the city. There are antique ceramics from Fajalauza, with blue and green designs of great beauty and originality, as well as curtains from Alpujarras, 17th-century furniture, wrought-iron work and a number of splendid copper pieces.

The museum also has a rich collection of courty pictures, including portraits of the Catholic Monarchs dating back to the 17th century, of Margaret of Austria, Philip IV, Isabel of Bourbon, Philip I, Philip II, John of Austria, Isabel of Farnesio and Philip V.

Entance archway to the Casa de Carbón. This building, dating back to the early 14th century, was used as a warehouse and lodgings for Moorish merchants.

However, the most outstanding work is the portrait of Charles V by Jerónimo de Chica. The attention of those admiring this room will also be drawn to the remarkable portraits of Boabdil and Aben-Humeya, and by the engravings of Moorish scenes.

A life-size figure of the slim and graceful Empress Eugenia of Montijo lends a special air to the room dedicated to her.

Another room, full of documentary and folkloric interest, is that devoted to the traditional customs of the Gypsies. The works displayed here include a curious collection of terracotta figures reproducing scenes from *Calé* life.

The many examples of the art of Granada on show in the various rooms of this museum lead us on a tour of discovery, revealing the history and the simple yet aristocratic crafts of the city.

The Albaicín: Church of San
Bartolomé

The Albaicín: Front of the
Convent of Santa Isabel la
Real.

◁ Courtyard of the Casa de
Carbón.

The Albaicín: Palace of
Daralhorra, or Casa de la
Reina.

A beautiful panoramic view of the Albaicín, seen from the Alhambra.

THE ALBAICIN

The Albaicín is a popular district of the city, with its own unique personality. During the time of Moorish rule, it was, with the Alcazaba, the most important centre of population in Granada. It stretches to the walls of the Alcazaba between this and Mount San Miguel on one side and to the Huadix and Alcaba gates on the other.

The name «Albaicín» probably derives from the fact that this part of the city was occupied by Moors settling here in 1227, having been driven out of Baeza by Ferdinand III, the Saint. Juan Rufo, in his poem «La Austriada», published in 1584, explains the change in spelling undergone by the name as follows: «*Y por ser de Baeza naturales los más de los que el sitio edificaron, llamáronle Albaecin, y otros no tales la «e» y la «c» en «y» y «z» mudaron*».

However, some researchers, such as the Arab scholar Aben Aljatib, consider that the name «Albaicín» means «the district on a slope or hill», which certainly matches the location of this delightful part of Granada.

Whatever the origin of its name, there is no doubt that the Albaicín was one of the busiest centres of population in Moorish Granada, a fact confirmed by its 30 or so mosques and the many public water tanks and fountains, many of which are still in existence today.

The people of Albaicín have always had a reputation for being proud and rebellious. Under Moorish rule, they would make raids in search of booty and, later on, when Granada had been reconquered by the Christian armies, they played an active part in the Moorish rebellion led by Aben Humeya, which ended in the expulsion of the vanquished rebels to Castile. This reverse marked the beginning of the decline of the Albaicín and of its industry, for Granadan textiles had enjoyed great fame during the Middle Ages. Nowadays, the Albaicín is a district which has retained much of its original simplicity. The interior of its houses evokes thoughts of its Moorish past, as does the veritable labyrinth of its narrow streets. The low houses cluster on the steep slopes, flanking irregular, narrow lanes with, as often as not, no pavements. To walk through the Albaicín today is to experience a strange sensation, of being submerged in an ancient world full of poetry and mystery. The distric commences on the Chapiz hill, from where there are wide, lovely views over the city. At its foot stretches the delightful Cármenes district, a charming combination of small dwellings and gardens which light up the entire area with harmonious strokes of vivid colour.

The Horatian charm of the «Carmenes», with its tiny houses and gardens, lends a feeling of peace and Christian humility to the Albaicín.

Church of San Pedro (16th century), Calle del Candil and the Morisca Chapiz House (15th-16th century).

THE SACROMONTE

Turning right off the old Guadix road, from the Casa del Chapiz, we come to the Sacromonte, bounded to the left by the Albaicín.

Climbing up towards the mountain, the road is bordered by cacti and prickly pears.

Suddenly, the caves appear before us, piercing deep into the mountain, and the bright, garish world of the Gypsies stands before us.

The caves are whitewashed inside and out, their walls covered with local pottery, copper pots and brightly-coloured paintings, an impressive array of local arts and culture.

The strumming of a guitar and the rhythmic click-click of the castanets is the musical accompaniment for the «jaleadores», who spur the dancers on with their clapping and shouting.

The statue of the Christ of the Gypsies arouses great fervour as it passes through the streets of Granada during the Holy Week celebrations.

Cristo de la Misericordia, by José de Mora.

HOLY WEEK

The religious festivals of Corpus Christi, declared by the Catholic Monarchs the official festival of Granada, and of Holy Week are celebrated with great pomp and splendour here, combining solemnity and spontaneity. Many *cofradías* (brotherhoods) file in procession through the streets of the city, carrying beautiful statues on *pasos* (floats), some of great artistic value and carved by such illustrious sculptors as Martínez Montañés, José de Mora or Pedro de Mena. Such works further exalt the solemnity of these celebrations. The devotion of the people fills the air with deep religious feeling, which overflow into fervour to create an unforgettable spectacle of colour on the day of the famous Gypsy procession. On Good Friday, the gathering of the faithful in the Campo del Príncipe forms a moving scene, equalling the impressive spectacle of the start of the procession led by the Virgen de las Angustias, patron saint of Granada.

The much-revered statue of Nuestra Señora de las Angustias passing through the Puerta de la Justicia in the Alhambra. The elegant combination of art and religion seem to endow the scene with a halo.

GASTRONOMY

Under the ironic even humour of the people of Granad lies a hidden vein of Eastern sensuality, manifested in many different, but nevertheless profound ways, and thus it is the Granada *cuisine* has retained the traditional elements of Muslim Andalusia, combining two original gastronomic sources, the Moorish and the Christian.

Varied and appetising are the typical dishes Granada offers to the palate of the gourmet. Among the finest are: Trevélez ham, cured in the cool air of the highest village in Spain, and eaten fried with delicious beans from the plains of Granada; omelette *al Sacromonte*; sardines *a la granadina;* exquisite almond soup or plain wheat broth. As an apperitive, what better than a slice of Trevélez ham washed down with a glass of noble wine from Huéscar, Huétor or Albandón.

As to desserts, Granada boasts a delicious and original variety, ranging from *huesos de santo* («Saint's bones») and *barretas,* to *empanadillas de Santa Catalina or tarta real* from Moorish Motril, *huevos moles de San Antón, batatines de San Bernardo* or classical *polverones de las Clarisas de Chauchina.* Not to forget, amongst the other excellent dishes too many to mention here, *borrachuelos, nochegüenos, voladillos* and *felipes.*

For desserts, Granada is truly the capital of Moorish-Andalusian *cuisine*.

Omelette al Sacromonte forms a persuasive argument in favour of Granadan cuisine.

Two well-known sweetmeats are huesos de santo («saint's bones») and barretas.

Views of the snow-capped mountains around Granada, showing a ski-lift and the Sierra Nevada Parador (National Hotel).

Three more views of the Sierra Nevada.

THE SIERRA NEVADA

The Sierra Nevada is the central chain in the Cordillera Bética. Its highest peaks are Mulhacén (3,478 metres) and Veleta (3,392).

Amongst the many accesses to these mountains is the Granada-Veleta road, the highest in Europe. At kilometre 14 is the Canales viewpoint, dominating a marvellous panorama.

There is a magnificent ski resort here, situated at around 2,100 metres above sea level and offering excellent hotel facilities. The area has been declared the «Solynieve Centre of National Tourist Interest». On the slopes of Mount Veleta perches the luxurious Parador (national hotel). Its privileged position means that visitors can enjoy winter sports practically the whole year round.

Mount Veleta: the Virgin of the Snows.

CONTENTS

Collection ALL EUROPE

#	Title	Spanish	French	English	German	Italian	Catalan	Dutch	Swedish	Portuguese	Japanese	Finnish
1	ANDORRA	•										
2	LISBON	•										
3	LONDON	•										
4	BRUGES	•										
5	PARIS	•										
6	MONACO	•										
7	VIENNA	•										
11	VERDUN	•										
12	THE TOWER OF LONDON	•										
13	ANTWERP	•										
14	WESTMINSTER ABBEY	•										
15	THE SPANISH RIDING SCHOOL IN VIENNA	•										
16	FATIMA	•										
17	WINDSOR CASTLE	•										
19	COTE D'AZUR	•										
22	BRUSSELS	•										
23	SCHÖNBRUNN PALACE	•										
24	ROUTE OF PORT WINE	•										
26	HOFBURG PALACE	•										
27	ALSACE	•										
31	MALTA											
32	PERPIGNAN											
33	STRASBOURG	•										
34	MADEIRA + PORTO SANTO											
35	CERDAGNE - CAPCIR											
36	BERLIN	•										

Collection ART IN SPAIN

#	Title	Spanish	French	English	German	Italian	Catalan	Dutch	Swedish	Portuguese	Japanese	Finnish
1	PALAU DE LA MUSICA CATALANA	•		•		•						
2	GAUDI	•	•	•	•						•	
3	PRADO MUSEUM I (Spanish Painting)	•	•	•	•	•					•	
4	PRADO MUSEUM II (Foreign Painting)	•	•	•	•	•						
5	MONASTERY OF GUADALUPE	•										
6	THE CASTLE OF XAVIER	•	•	•	•						•	
7	THE FINE ARTS MUSEUM OF SEVILLE	•	•	•	•	•						
8	SPANISH CASTLES	•	•	•	•							
9	THE CATHEDRALS OF SPAIN	•	•	•	•							
10	THE CATHEDRAL OF GERONA	•										
14	PICASSO	•	•	•	•	•					•	
15	REALES ALCAZARES (ROYAL PALACE OF SEVILLE)	•	•	•	•	•						
16	MADRID'S ROYAL PALACE	•	•	•	•	•						
17	ROYAL MONASTERY OF EL ESCORIAL	•	•	•	•	•						
18	THE WINES OF CATALONIA	•	•	•	•							
19	THE ALHAMBRA AND THE GENERALIFE	•	•	•	•	•						
20	GRANADA AND THE ALHAMBRA	•										
21	ROYAL ESTATE OF ARANJUEZ	•	•	•	•	•						
22	ROYAL ESTATE OF EL PARDO	•	•	•	•	•						
23	ROYAL HOUSES	•	•	•	•	•						
24	ROYAL PALACE OF SAN ILDEFONSO	•	•	•	•	•						
25	HOLY CROSS OF THE VALLE DE LOS CAIDOS	•	•	•	•	•						
26	OUR LADY OF THE PILLAR OF SARAGOSSA	•	•	•								
27	TEMPLE DE LA SAGRADA FAMILIA	•	•	•	•	•	•					
28	POBLET ABTEI	•	•	•			•					

Collection ALL SPAIN

#	Title	Spanish	French	English	German	Italian	Catalan	Dutch	Swedish	Portuguese	Japanese	Finnish
1	ALL MADRID	•	•	•	•	•					•	
2	ALL BARCELONA	•	•	•	•	•	•	•				
3	ALL SEVILLE	•	•	•	•	•					•	
4	ALL MAJORCA	•	•	•	•	•		•				
5	ALL THE COSTA BRAVA	•	•	•	•	•	•					
6	ALL MALAGA and the Costa del Sol	•	•	•	•	•	•		•			
7	ALL THE CANARY ISLANDS (Gran Canaria)	•	•	•	•	•	•	•	•			
8	ALL CORDOBA	•	•	•	•	•	•				•	
9	ALL GRANADA	•	•	•	•	•	•					
10	ALL VALENCIA	•	•	•	•	•	•					
11	ALL TOLEDO	•	•	•	•	•	•				•	
12	ALL SANTIAGO	•	•	•	•	•	•					
13	ALL IBIZA and Formentera	•	•	•	•	•	•					
14	ALL CADIZ and the Costa de la Luz	•	•	•	•	•						
15	ALL MONTSERRAT	•	•	•	•	•	•					
16	ALL SANTANDER and Cantabria	•	•									
17	ALL THE CANARY ISLANDS II, (Tenerife)	•	•	•	•	•			•	•		•
20	ALL BURGOS	•	•	•	•	•						
21	ALL ALICANTE and the Costa Blanca	•	•	•	•	•	•	•				
22	ALL NAVARRA	•	•	•	•							
23	ALL LERIDA	•	•	•			•					
24	ALL SEGOVIA	•	•	•	•							
25	ALL SARAGOSSA	•	•	•	•	•						
26	ALL SALAMANCA	•	•	•	•	•				•		
27	ALL AVILA	•	•	•	•	•	•					
28	ALL MINORCA	•										
29	ALL SAN SEBASTIAN and Guipúzcoa	•										
30	ALL ASTURIAS	•		•								
31	ALL LA CORUNNA and the Rías Altas	•	•	•	•	•	•					
32	ALL TARRAGONA	•	•	•	•	•	•					
33	ALL MURCIA	•	•	•	•							
34	ALL VALLADOLID	•	•	•	•							
35	ALL GIRONA	•	•	•								
36	ALL HUESCA	•	•									
37	ALL JAEN	•	•	•	•							
38	ALL ALMERIA	•	•	•	•							
40	ALL CUENCA	•	•	•	•							
41	ALL LEON	•	•	•	•	•						
42	ALL PONTEVEDRA, VIGO and the Rías Bajas	•	•	•	•	•	•					
43	ALL RONDA	•	•	•	•	•	•					
44	ALL SORIA	•										
46	ALL EXTREMADURA	•										
47	ALL ANDALUSIA	•	•	•	•				•			
52	ALL MORELLA	•	•		•							

Collection ALL AMERICA

#	Title	Spanish	French	English	German	Italian	Catalan	Dutch	Swedish	Portuguese	Japanese	Finnish
1	PUERTO RICO	•		•								
2	SANTO DOMINGO	•										
3	QUEBEC		•	•								
4	COSTA RICA	•		•								
5	CARACAS	•										

Collection ALL AFRICA

#	Title	Spanish	French	English	German	Italian	Catalan	Dutch	Swedish	Portuguese	Japanese	Finnish
1	MOROCCO	•	•	•	•	•						
2	THE SOUTH OF MOROCCO	•	•	•	•	•						
3	TUNISIA		•	•	•	•						
4	RWANDA	•